My First
BOOK OF MORMON
Activity Book

VOLUME TWO ALMA-MORONi

LAURA LEE ROSTROM

ISBN 13: 978-1-59955-958-2

Published by CFI, an imprint of Cedar Fort, Inc.
2373 W. 700 S., Springville, UT, 84663
Distributed by Cedar Fort, Inc., www.cedarfort.com

Cover and page design by Rebecca Jensen
Cover design © 2012 by Lyle Mortimer

Printed in the United States of America

10 9 8 7 6 5 4 3

Printed on acid-free paper

Ammon was a missionary.

He served the Lamanite King
by watching his sheep.

Which two sheep are the same?

But mean men kept
scattering the sheep away.

Ammon stopped the mean
men and saved the sheep!

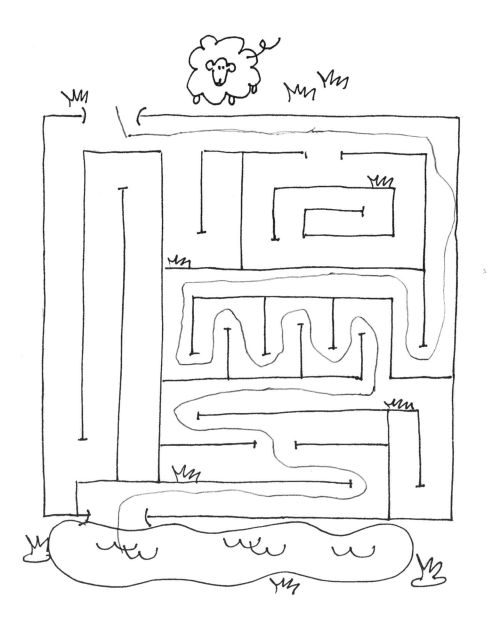

Help the sheep find the watering hole.

Word Search

A	M	C	E	G	I	K	M	O	A
Q	I	S	U	W	Y	A	C	E	B
B	S	D	F	H	J	L	N	P	I
R	S	T	V	X	Z	A	S	C	S
K	I	N	G	E	G	I	H	K	H
M	O	O	P	Q	U	E	E	N	R
S	N	T	V	L	W	Y	E	A	C
B	A	M	M	O	N	D	P	F	H
I	R	K	M	V	O	Q	S	U	V
X	Y	Z	R	E	J	E	S	U	S

Can you find these words?

LOVE   KING
AMMON   QUEEN
SHEEP   ABISH
JESUS   MISSIONARY

7

The king thought Ammon
was a great spirit.

Connect the dots.

Ammon told the king about
Jesus, and the King believed him.

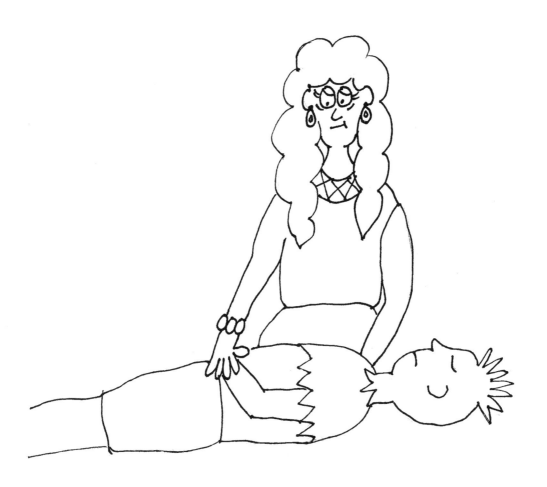

The king felt terrible for being so bad.
He fell to the ground.

Later on, the queen fell
to the ground too.

Can you match what
belongs together?

Abish, the queen's helper,
already believed in Jesus.
She knew they would wake up.

The king told his people about Jesus.
Many of them believed and rejoiced.

They were filled with love.

How many hearts do you count? _6_

Can you draw more hearts?

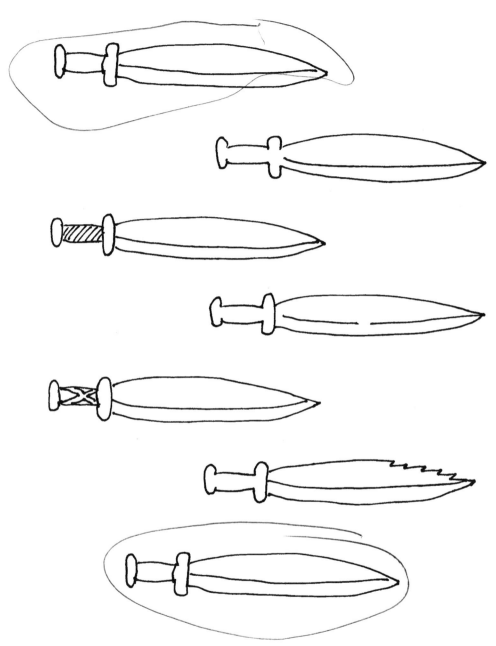

Which two swords are the same?

They buried all their weapons and
promised never to fight again.

Captain Moroni was a great leader.

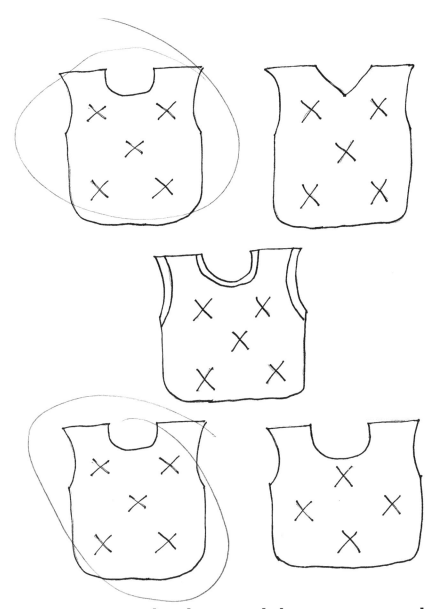

He taught his soldiers to make
metal breastplates for protection.

Which two are the same?

In memory of our
God, our religion,
and freedom, and
our peace, our wives,
and our children.

Captain Moroni made a title of
liberty to go on every tower.

Can you draw a flag on every tower?

Captain Moroni was a great leader.

He was ...

Rude   Righteous   Mean   Loud

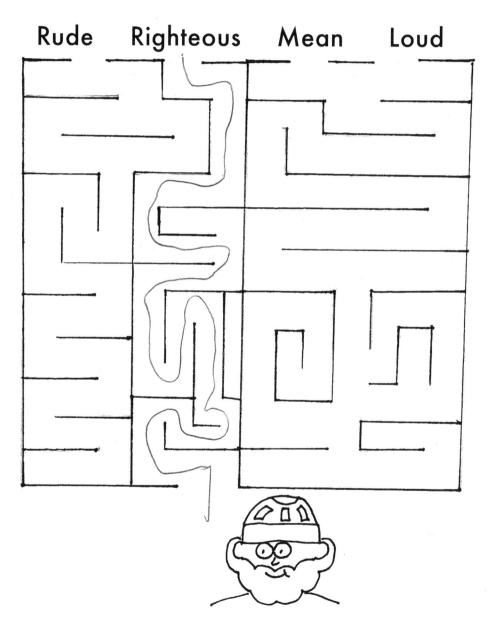

Cross Word Puzzle

3D f a m i l i e s

1D

2A | f | r | e | e | d | o | m |

1A | l | e | a | d | e | r |

3A | l | i | b | e | r | t | y |

4D M o r o n i

4A | p | l | a | t | e | s |

2D t o w e r

Across

1. Captain Moroni was a great _____.
2. He wanted his people to have _____.
3. He made a title of _____.
4. For protection, his soldiers made metal breast _____.

Down

1. Captain Moroni made a _____.
2. He put it on every _____.
3. He wanted to protect _____.
4. The Nephites rallied behind Captain _____.

Helaman was also a great leader,
but he needed more soldiers.

The people baptized by Ammon
promised to never fight again,
but they wanted to help.

Their sons did not promise,
so they became soldiers.
There were two thousand sons!

Circle the number 2000

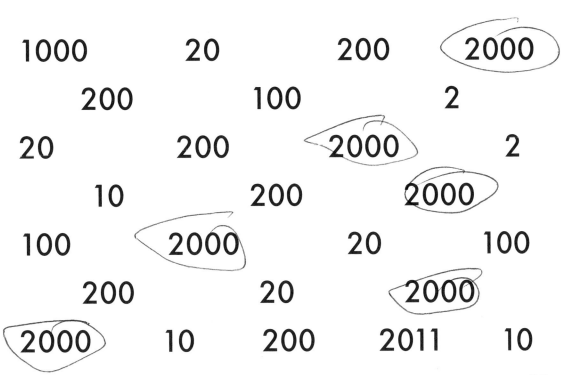

1000   20   200   2000

          200   100   2

20   200   2000   2

          10   200   2000

100   2000   20   100

          200   20   2000

2000   10   200   2011   10

Can you write the number 2,000?

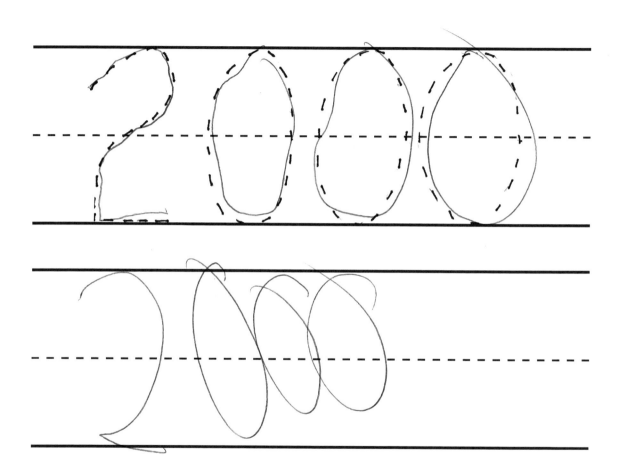

Help Helaman's stripling warriors surround the city.

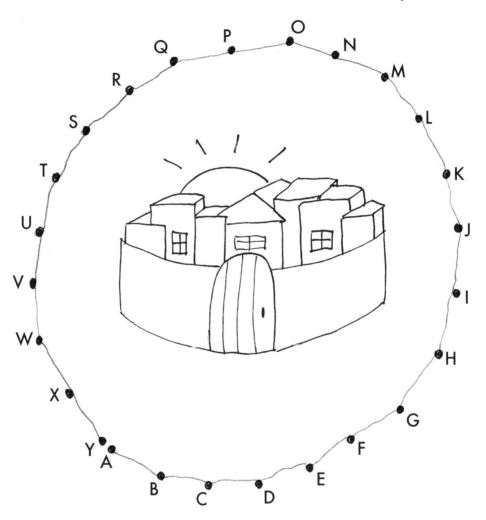

Connect the dots.

The stripling
warriors
were
fearless.

Their mothers taught that
God would protect them.
They all survived the battle.

Can you draw a picture of
you with your mother?

Word Search

```
A C H E L A M A N F
M B D F H J L N P E
O W A R R I O R S A
T Q S U W Y A C E R
H P R O M I S E G L
E I K M O Q S U W E
R Y B D F H J L N S
S T R I P L I N G S
Q O B S O L D I E R
X P R O T E C T D F
```

Can you find these words?

HELAMAN
STRIPLING
WARRIORS
FEARLESS

MOTHERS
SOLDIER
PROMISE
PROTECT

30

Cross Word Puzzle

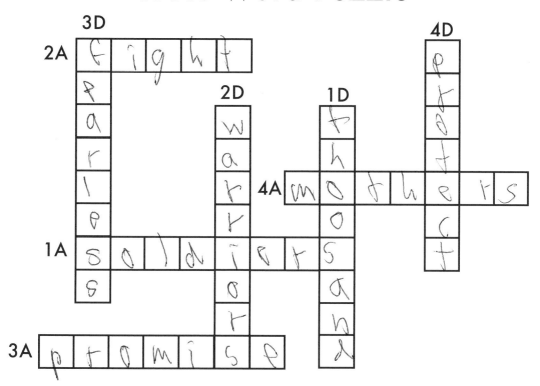

Across

1. Helaman needed more _____.

2. The people of Ammon promised to never _____.

3. But their sons did not make this _____.

4. They were taught by their _____.

Down

1. Their sons numbered two _____.

2. Helaman called them his stripling _____.

3. They were _____.

4. Their mothers taught that God would _____ them.

31

Samuel the Lamanite was a prophet.

Help Samuel find his way to the Nephites.

START

NEPHITES

The Lord wanted Samuel to
give the Nephites a message.
He told them that the Son of
God would be born soon.

Some people believed Samuel, but some did not. The unbelievers threw stones and shot arrows at him.

Can you draw arrows and
stones missing Samuel?

He was safe!

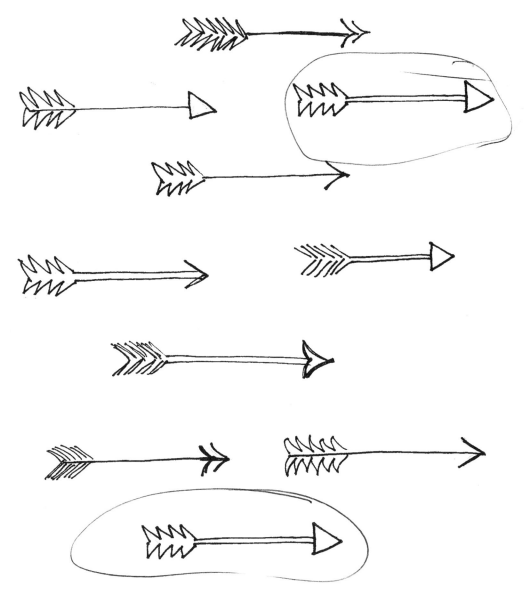

Circle the two arrows that are the same.

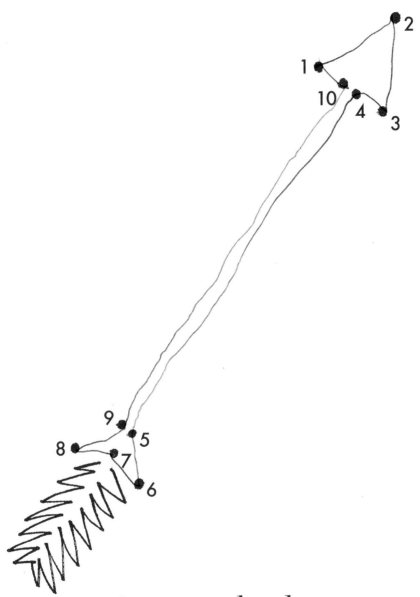

Connect the dots.

Many prophets taught that
Jesus would be born on earth.

They said a new star would shine and
the night would be bright like day.

Color the stars with four points.
How many did you color? _____7_____

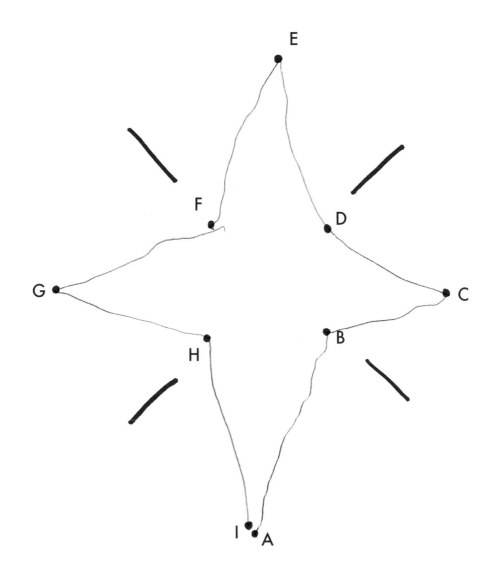

Connect the dots.

It is a __S__ __T__ __A__ __R__ .

The believers were so happy
when they saw the new star.

They knew Jesus was
born on the earth.

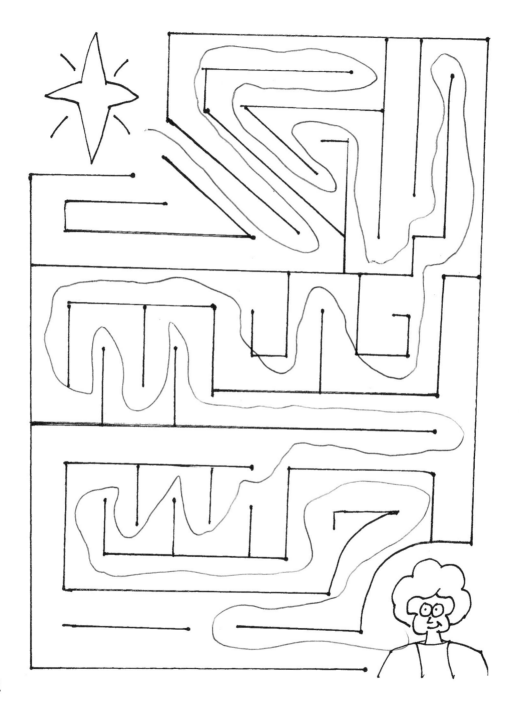

Word Search

```
Z X S T A R M O Q S
B M A O Q S U W Y P
I Z M A R R O W S R
R A U C E G I K M O
T N E S T O N E Q P
H O L P Q S U W L H
B E L I E V E R S E
X J E S U S Z A C T
R T V X Z A C E G I
J L N P R T V X Z A
```

Can you find these words?

STAR

SAMUEL

ARROWS

STONE

BELIEVERS

PROPHET

JESUS

BIRTH

45

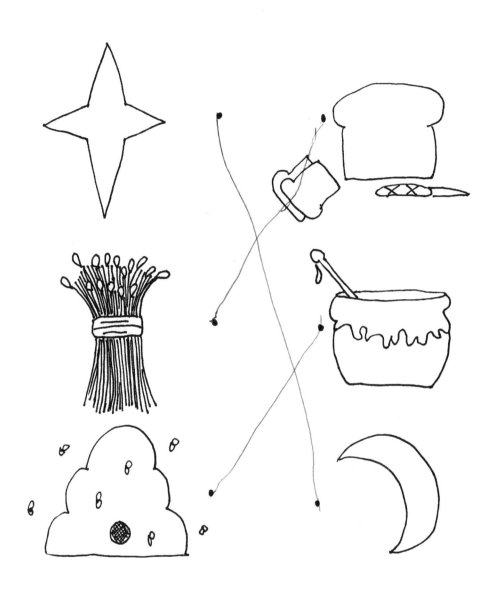

Match what belongs together.

Cross Word Puzzle

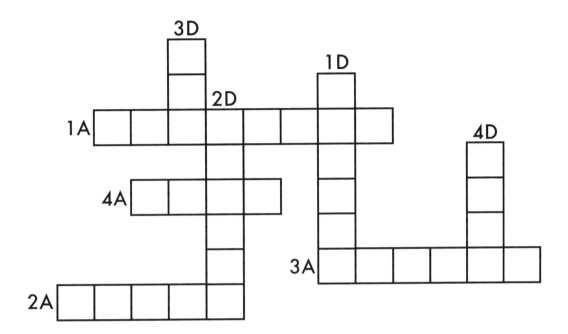

Across

1. Samuel was a _____.
2. He told the Nephites about the birth of _____.
3. Some Nephites believed _____.
4. Some did not believe Jesus would be _____.

Down

1. The unbelievers threw _____.
2. They also shot _____ at him.
3. But not one hit _____.
4. Samuel was _____.

The Lord asked the brother of
Jared to build eight barges to
sail to a new land.

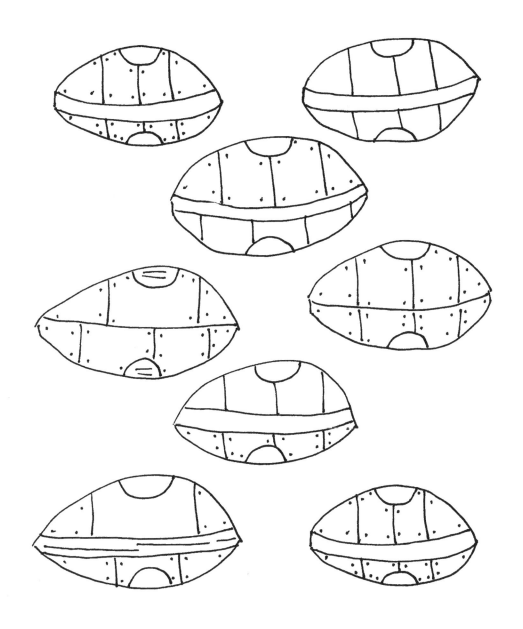

Which two barges are the same?

The brother of Jared wondered how
he would light the barges. Fire would
burn the wood, so he cut clear stones.

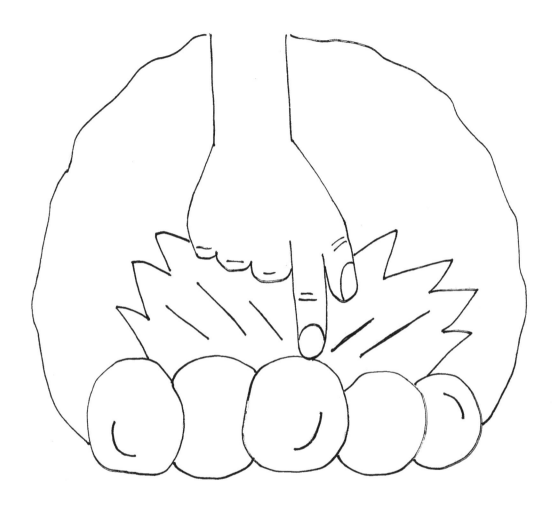

The brother of Jared asked the Lord to touch each stone and make them shine bright.

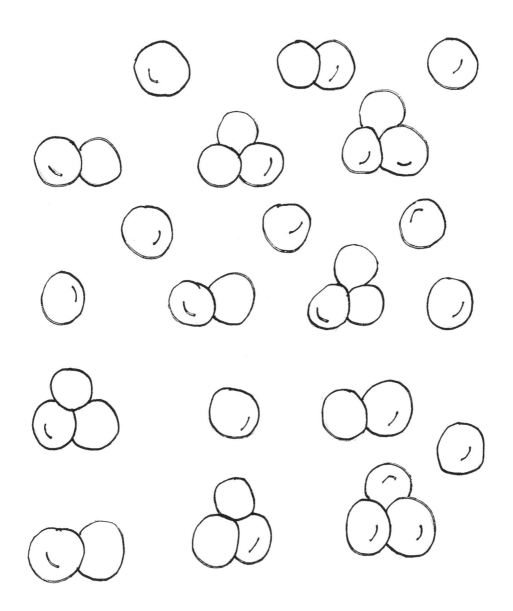

Circle each pile with two stones.

He was surprised to see the
finger of the Lord. He did not
know Jesus had a body.

Jesus said, "Because of your
faith, you can see me."

Word Search

B A J A R E D B D F
A G I K F M O Q R S
R T V X A Y C Z A H
G B D F I H L J L I
E M O Q T R E S U N
S V X Z H B A C D E
S T O N E S R F H I
J L N P R T V X Z A
B D F I N G E R E G
L I G H T H J L N D

Can you find these words?

BARGES   FINGER
JARED   SHINE
LIGHT   FAITH
STONES   CLEAR

Match what belongs together.

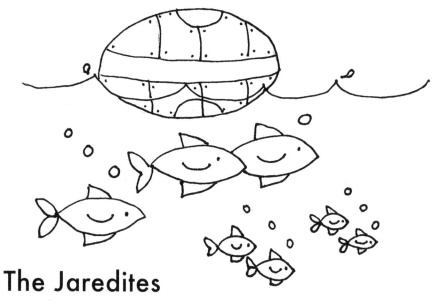

The Jaredites
traveled the sea
for many days.

Can you find this fish?

Count the starfish. _____

58

Color the spaces with a dot.

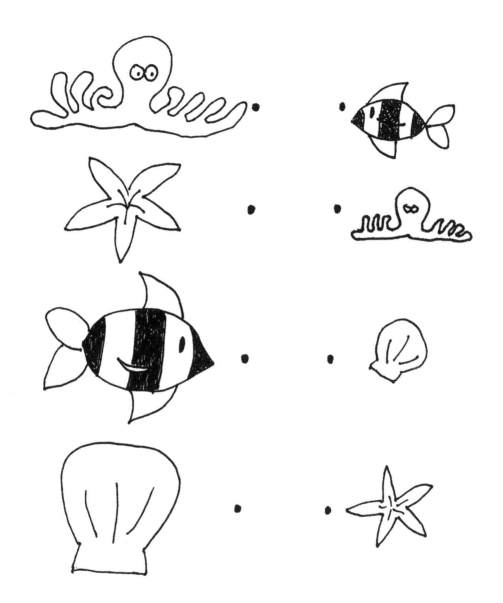

Match what belongs together.

FINISH

START

Help the Jaredites find their new land.

The Jaredites were grateful for their new home.

Find a turtle, deer, mouse, swan, snake, rabbit, butterfly, crab, fish, and two birds.